ISBN-10: 1544660804
ISBN-13: 978-1544660806

the words i want you to keep

GABY COMPRÉS

these words are for you

i have dreamed of this day for years. of you holding this
book in your hands.
here it is. here we are.
and it's everything i hoped it would be.
i hope these words are what you hoped they'd be.
i hope these words speak to you. i hope they awake your
bones. i hope they make you smile and cry happy tears.
i hope you read them when you're happy. i hope you read
them when you're sad.
i hope you find yourself in these pages.
i hope you find the things i poured in them: love, hope,
bravery and light.
i hope you keep them, because they are for you.
these are the words i want you to keep.
i want you to keep them like a song that stays stuck in
your head.
i want you to keep them,
to keep their truth,
to believe that there is light and goodness in you.
these are the words i want you to keep.
i hope you do.

gaby comprés

to whom it may concern

my words are for you.

this is me giving you light,
kindling a fire in your heart,
grabbing your hands and holding them in my own,
looking you in the eye,
and telling you i believe there's so much more.
so much more for your eyes to see,
so many places your feet haven't known.
so much more.

this is me telling you
i refuse to believe that this is it,
i refuse to believe that the stars don't shine for us,
that the beating of our hearts is a song that
will go by unheard.

this is me telling you
i choose to believe your life is an unfolding story,
i choose to believe you are a work of art,
a masterpiece in the making.

my words are for you.

there is more to you that you have yet to know

there are stars you
haven't seen
and loves you haven't loved
there's light you haven't felt
and sunrises yet to dawn
there are dreams
you haven't dreamt
and days you haven't lived
and nights you won't forget
and flowers yet to grow
and there is more to you
that you have yet to
know.

you are loved

your life is more than life.
it is light and fire
and bravery and hope and a song.
and you are loved.

hope is the song of your heart // for Charissa

hope is the song of your heart,
even if you've forgotten the words.
its melody runs through your veins,
it lives in your soul, in your bones.
hope is the song of your heart,
and even when the waves tried to drown you,
and the darkness tried to dim your light,
your heart still sang its song.
hope is the song of your heart,
and you will remember the words.
and when you do,
i'll be next to you to sing along.

bravery makes your feet dance

your eyes are bright,
as if they held
constellations inside,
as if your soul were the sky.
your heart holds dreams
you have yet to dream
and songs of love and hope.
bravery stirs
and dances inside you,
reminding you she hasn't left;
she is still here.
you are still here,
lost,
but you'll find the way,
because you hold the stars
in your eyes
and bravery makes your feet dance.

you don't have to carry what doesn't belong to you

the lies you've believed
are not yours.
the shame you've carried
is not yours.
the words that hurt you,
the mistakes you made,
they are not yours.
the number on the scale,
the brokenness you carry,
they're not yours.
be still. let go.
you don't have to carry
what doesn't belong to you.

gaby comprés

yours

yours is the sun,
the moon
and every single star.
yours is a brand-new day,
the belief that good things
are on their way.
yours is the spring
that follows the winter,
the rain that waters new life.
yours is grace,
yours is redemption,
yours are my words.

we are beautiful

we have stars in our eyes and fire in our souls and dreams in our hearts. we have songs in our heads and stories to tell. we have broken hearts that learn to heal over and over again and shattered dreams and lost loves and failed friendships. we have tear-stained cheeks and memories of endless nights.

we are beautiful.

we are heavy and we are light and we are dark and yet so bright. we carry burdens and joy. we have songs of laughter and rivers of tears. we have words to write and tell and melodies to sing. we have grace and redemption gluing our broken pieces together and somehow making them more beautiful than when we were whole.

we are beautiful.

we are alive. we are beautiful. we have glory tangled in our hair. we are the most beautiful mess. we are unsure and certain and vulnerable and strong. we know what we want but we fear it too. we are sinners and saints and sunrises and sunsets.

we are beautiful.

we are beautiful, for we are so much more than flesh and
bones. we are bravery, we are songs. we are reflections of
glory. we are beautiful, for we have dreams and wild and
beating hearts.

we are beautiful, for we are more light than we are dark.
we are more than what we know, more than what we
dream, more than who we are in this very moment. we are
not who we will be. we have hope. we have grace. we have
beauty.

we are beautiful.

el cielo te quiere saludar

mira pa' arriba,
que el cielo te quiere saludar.
te quiere decir que el sol brilla solo para ti,
y las nubes te mandan besos de algodón.
mira pa' arriba,
que vienen días mejores,
llenos de luz.
mira pa' arriba,
no pierdas la esperanza.
descubre la belleza que se esconde en tus días,
todo lo hermoso que hay es para ti.
mira pa' arriba
y deja que el sol te bese.
mira pa' arriba
y sigue adelante.

the sky wants to say hello

look up, the sky wants to say hello.
it wants to tell you that the sun shines for you
and that the clouds send you cotton candy kisses.
look up, better days are coming,
filled with joy and light.
look up, don't lose hope.
find the beauty that lives in your days,
everything that is beautiful was made for you.
look up, and let the sun kiss you.
look up, and keep going forward.

the words i want you to keep

hope is mine

hope is mine.
it lives in me, even when it feels like i have lost it.
hope is mine, because my soul craves it every day.
my heartbeat is a song of hope.
every time my heart drums, it tells me i am still here.
i still have hope.
even when i don't think i do. even when i can't find my
words.
even if i feel lost and small.
even if the waves are too strong and i can't fight them.
even when joy hides a little too well from me.
love is on his way. hope is on his way.
He will knock on the doors of my heart, and sit on the
chairs of my soul.
and He will wipe my tears, and call me redeemed and
beloved.
He will make it rain, and the spring my heart longs for will
come.
but in the meantime, i will celebrate.
i will celebrate my smallness, even when i don't want to,
because my smallness leaves room for grace.
i will celebrate the beauty around me and inside me.
i will let the daylight in.
i will place flowers on my head, symbols of beauty and
glory and grace.
and hope.

i hope you find yourself

i hope you find yourself
under skies of blue and pink
and orange and purple and
i hope you find yourself
smiling when it rains and
i hope you find yourself
among beautiful things
and that you think that
you're beautiful too and
i hope you find yourself
running free and redeemed,
certain of your worth and
i hope you find yourself
among the dancing night stars,
shining brighter than all of them and
i hope you find yourself
on mountaintops, gazing at
the world before you with
hopeful eyes, and
i hope you find yourself
letting go of your pain and
i hope you find yourself
with grace and love and hope
tangled around your soul and
i hope you find yourself.

let's be

let's be wild and brave
and tender and soft
and bright and sweet and
lovely and free
and let's be
stars and galaxies and stardust
and little bits of light
and let's be
wonderful and beautiful
and small and yet too big
and strong but vulnerable
and let's be
diamonds and dust
and dreamers and fighters
and fire and joy and grace
let's be you and me.

come closer

come closer,
look inside, and don't be afraid
of what you might find.
travel down
the roads of your soul,
until you know by heart
every corner and place of your being.
learn your fears so you may know how
to fight them,
and gaze at your skies
and try to number the millions of stars
in your heart,
and trace with your hands
every bit of who you are,
and know yourself
so you may not forget yourself,
and your worth,
and the constellations of grace and light
inside you.
do not forget yourself,
do not ignore the melody of your heart,
do not doubt your beauty, your worth,
and the bits of glory and stardust sprinkled
on your skin.
come closer.

a list of the things my soul forgot

i am still brave
i am free
i am beautiful
i have hope
i am redeemed
i am alive
and my story is still being written
i am worth more than the words i write
and i have worth even when i cannot write
and i am also worth more than the sun
and the moon
and the stars
i can dream
i am not perfect and it is okay to struggle
because even though i don't deserve grace
it is mine
i am lovely
and i am loved
and even if i forget the truth
that doesn't change that
it is still true.

tu historia aquí no acaba

vas a ver, que todo pasa.
que la tormenta cesará,
y el mar se calmará
y el sol saldrá de nuevo para ti.
ya verás, que todo pasa,
que tus pies no están estancados
y volverás a andar
y volverás a cantar tu canción.
todo pasa,
y aunque sea de noche,
brillarán las estrellas hasta
que salga el sol.
vas a ver, que todo pasa;
que tu historia aquí no acaba.

this is not the end of your story

you will see, this will pass.
the storm will end
and the sun will come out again.
you will see, this will pass.
your feet aren't stuck
and they will walk again
and you will sing your song.
this will pass,
and even though it is dark,
in your sky the stars will shine
until the sun comes back.
you will see, this will pass.
this is not the end of your story.

no te olvides

no te olvides.
no dejes que las olas del tiempo
te arrastren a ti,
arrastren tus sueños.
no te dejes perder.
y si el mar insiste,
deja que lo único
que las olas se lleven
sean tus miedos y tus tristezas.
no te pierdas.
y si te llegas a perder,
piérdete en las estrellas,
hasta que brilles como ellas,
hasta que seas luz.
no te olvides,
no olvides los pasos que diste,
las palabras que oíste
y todo lo que viviste
para llegar hasta aquí.
y si te llegas a olvidar,
detente a escuchar
el latido de tu corazón,
aquella canción
que dice que no te has ido,
que estás aquí, que no te olvides.

do not forget yourself

do not forget yourself.
don't let the waves of time
drag you,
don't let them drag your dreams.
don't lose yourself.
but if the sea rages,
let the waves take only
your fears and sorrows.
don't lose yourself.
but if you lose your way,
lose yourself in the stars,
until you shine like them,
until you become light.

i am

i am magic.
i am the night sky and every single star,
i am the ocean and every ripple and wave.
i am a house of flesh and bone,
of hope and freedom.
i am a bird,
wild and free,
i am everything i dream of being.
i am a song,
a song of bravery and love,
of light and gold.
i am a voice that is not unheard;
my words are not shouted off into a void.
i am my heart, my words, my love.
i am known,
i am loved.

i love me like this

i love me like this,
with the night in my eyes
and the cinnamon moon
that sits atop my nose.
i love me like this,
with my wild and untamable curls,
who only listen to the wind.
i love me like this,
with my skin that matches
the *café con leche* i love to drink.
i love me like this,
with my poetry and without her;
with the words i feel
and the words i've kept to myself.
i love me like this,
light and free;
because this is who i am,
this is who i was made to be.

me quiero así

me quiero así,
con mis ojos color noche
y mi nariz redonda
y la luna de canela que vive sobre ella.
me quiero así,
con mi pelo rizado e indomable
que solo se deja llevar por el viento.
me quiero así,
con mi piel del mismo color
del café con leche
que me gusta tanto.
me quiero así,
con mi poesía y sin ella,
con las palabras que siento,
con las palabras que callo.
me quiero así,
mágica y única;
porque así soy,
porque así me hicieron,
porque sí.

stories

we all are stories,
we are books longing for someone
to look beyond our covers,
and turn our pages
and read the ink tattooed on them.
we long to be seen,
we want to be read and understood
and loved,
we are hoping to become poetry
to those hearts that see us,
something beautiful and unforgettable.

i want a love

i want a love
that tastes like honey,
a love that caresses my skin
and lets its fingers get tangled in my hair.
i want a love
that doesn't read my mind
but my heart; a love that knows
the nooks and crannies of my soul.
i want a love
that smells like coffee and roses,
a love that doesn't give up
and seeks freedom.
i want a love
that is poetry, with rhyming promises,
free verses and words of love.
i want a love
that sees me as i am;
a love that won't let my light fade.
i want a love
that loves me.

your smile // for Nicole

your smile
is the sun, the moon,
the stars
and every bit
of light

you've always had wings //
for Rafaella

may you learn to be brave
and may you always run carefree,
certain of your worth and the power inside you.
may your song be your own,
and when your song is different from the rest,
sing louder.
may you never forget that you've always had wings,
and may they carry you far.

a blessing

when the morning comes,
may you smile at the sun,
and may its light touch your heart.
when the morning comes,
may the birds sing to you songs of hope.
when the morning comes,
may you find the grace your heart needs.
when the morning comes,
may joy light the way before you.

my heart beats in poetry

this heart, my heart,
beats in poetry,
in words for you,
words for me.
this heart beats
words of hope and light
to fight the darkness.
this heart beats
in words that are born at midnight,
words mothered by late-night coffee
words i didn't know i kept inside
until i wrote them out.
this heart, my heart,
beats in poetry
because it doesn't know
how else to beat,
because it doesn't know
how else to feel,
because it doesn't know
how to let out everything i keep inside.
this heart beats in poetry
for you,
for me.

a story

there is a story
written on your skin;
a story that grows
with every sunrise,
a story filled with light
and darkness,
peppered with freckles
and scars.
there is a story
written on your skin,
a story that tells the world
that you are still here,
that you're not leaving;
a story of wonder
and grace,
redemption and joy.
a story of bitter and sweet,
of love and heaven.
there is a story
written on your skin,
a story of hope,
a story yours alone.

a ladder

let's build a ladder, you and i.
a ladder taller than
skyscrapers and towers.
a ladder so high we can reach the stars
and grab them and keep them in our souls
to fight away the darkness.
a ladder so tall,
higher than sorrow and pain.
a ladder so high
that when we reach the top,
you and i feel infinite and small at the
same time and maybe even
have a taste at glory
when we look down at the world.
let's build a ladder, you and i.
let's climb our way home.

in places that are too small

my knees tremble
and my throat turns dry
and i mess up my words
and i forget what i want to say
sometimes
but it feels a million times
righter than hiding
behind masks
and comfort zones
and security
and being just a shadow of who i am
in my sleep,
of who i am in my dreams,
because my soul knows
i was made for more than to simply settle,
more than giving up, more than squeezing
my soul
and my heart
and who i am
in places that are too small.

gaby comprés

pretty

you say that when i'm skinny
i'll be pretty,
but don't you see that now
i smile easily,
and my eyes look like the stars?
don't you see that my laughter
sounds like a song,
and my feet are lighter
and nothing weighs me down?
you say i will be pretty,
but don't you see that i already am,
that i always have been?
don't you see i am much more than
pretty,
that i am someone with dreams,
with hope and light?

bonita

dices que cuando sea más flaca
seré bonita,
¿pero tú no ves
que ahora
la sonrisa me sale más fácil,
que mis ojos parecen estrellas,
que mi felicidad no es fingida?
¿no te das cuenta
de que mi risa parece música,
que mis pies bailan,
que nada me pesa?
dices que voy a ser bonita,
¿pero no ves que ya lo soy,
que siempre lo fui?
¿no ves que soy mucho más que eso,
que estoy llena de sueños,
llena de vida,
llena de esperanza y luz?

gaby comprés

i will always be her

i will always be her,
this girl with the wild curls
and the gentle eyes
that look for poetry in the sunset sky,
and i will always be her,
this girl with bravery
seeping into my bones,
with freedom tattooed on my skin.
i will always be her,
this girl with a heart
full of dreams and hope,
and words to write.
i will always be her,
this girl with a soul too big,
a light too bright.
i will always be her,
and she can't be taken away from me.

ella

a ella le gusta la música del mar,
y las letras con poesía.
le gusta sentirse libre,
enamorada de la vida.
le gusta que el viento se enrede en su pelo,
y encontrar poesía en el cielo.
ella ama la luz,
del sol, de las estrellas.
ella se quiere, así como es,
valiente y asustada,
simple y complicada,
con el alma tan grande que no la puede esconder.

she loves

she loves the music of the waves,
and the poetry in music.
she loves to feel free,
to feel in love with life.
she loves it when the wind gets tangled in her hair,
and finding poetry in the sky.
she loves the light
of the sun and of the stars.
and she loves herself, the way she is:
brave and scared,
simple and complicated,
with a soul so big she can't hide it.

the words I want you to keep

my Caribbean sea

paint me the color of
my Caribbean sea,
a wild but peaceful blue
sing to me the music of
my Caribbean sea,
the waves that call me to be still
dance with me to the tune of
my Caribbean sea,
a waltz of giving and taking,
like the mingling of water and sand
take me to
my Caribbean sea,
where my dreams are cradled by the cerulean waves,
where my bones first learned to dance,
here in my Caribbean sea

brokenness is not where your story ends

oh my soul,
these bones and heart of yours
have been broken for glory, for light,
by grace.
they are turning into art and stardust,
into more, into something wilder
than your wildest dreams,
into a song that will wake the sleepers.
they will tell a story of redemption and glory
and the most beautiful love.
oh my soul,
brokenness is not where your story ends.

buy yourself bright flowers pt. i

i buy flowers because hope lives in them.

flowers begin as seeds. they're buried in the earth. they
need sun and rain and time to grow. it takes time and
effort before flowers begin to bloom. winter must end and
spring must arrive. and when spring comes, glory shines
down on those flowers and they bloom. they show their
majestic and bright and colorful petals.

and i guess life's a lot like a flower. there are tears and
hard days and dark and rainy nights and pain. and time
passes and it feels like you're stuck in the same season
and that you'll be stuck forever. and you don't see it, but
the bittersweet of your season changes you. it makes you
stronger. it makes you brave. it teaches you lessons. it
makes you grow. and then your spring comes, and just
like the flowers, you bloom, and the world gets to see who
you've been all along. they see your glorious and beauti-
ful petals. they see the wonderful being that you are. you
bloom, and you see that you are not who you were. your
soul grows as big and bright as a sunflower's petals and
you find that it no longer fits where you used to fit, that
you can no longer be a small seed hiding in the earth. you
uncover the art and the beauty and the glory that have
always lived in you.

buy yourself bright flowers. buy them and keep them
in your room, so that every time you see them you may
remember that you're as bright and lovely as they are. buy
them so that they remind you of who you'll be, of who you
are: bright and bold and gorgeous and unfolding.
buy them to remember that you too will bloom.

inside you

inside you,
there are oceans and rivers
and streams of light.
inside you,
live butterflies and songbirds
making sweet music and beauty.
inside you, there are galaxies
and constellations and shooting stars
and a little bit of magic.
inside you,
there are meadows of sunflowers
and fields of wildflowers and gold.
inside you,
there are stories waiting to be told
and stories that haven't happened yet
and inside you, there is bravery and
love and laughter and hope and light
and wonder and grace and summer
and spring
and a million little things
that make you
you.

like this, right now

like this. right now.

you are loved.

completely.

wonderfully.

loved.

wildly.

relentlessly.

loved.

unconditionally.

unwaveringly.

loved.

like this. right now.

your love is mine

your love
flows like a river
your love is a song
i want to hear
again and again and again
your love is like
drops of rain
your love
gets tangled in my soul
and gets caught between my fingers
like thread
your love is my milk and honey
my bread and wine
the stars of my sky
and the flowers of my spring
your love is mine.

remember me

remember me like this,
with a smile on my face,
with a spark in my eyes,
with my words
dripping down my hands
like honey,
hoping to sweeten your days.
remember me like this,
quiet and thinking,
wanting to keep this moment forever.
remember me.

we forgot

darkness came upon us
and we forgot
the dancing stars that live inside our bones
we forgot the seeds of hope
that were planted in our souls
we forgot to listen to our music,
to the drums of our beating hearts
we forgot our beauty
we forgot our worth
but our hearts keep beating
and our souls still sing
and if we dare to listen
those seeds of hope will bloom
and those stars inside us
will show us the way back home.

remember to hope

(remember) to turn on the light
when your days become too dark.
remember the beautiful things your eyes have seen;
the cotton candy clouds,
the fields of wildflowers
the stars that dance in the sky.
turn on the light
and hold on (to hope).

the words i want you to keep

i hope for you

i think of you
as i write these words,
the words i want you to keep.
and i hope for you.
i hope that you are happy,
that you find what you are looking for,
i hope that you grow,
that you get to know your soul.
i hope Love finds you,
and that you learn to savor
the bittersweet of life,
the rain and sunshine,
the winter and spring.
i hope there's a lighthouse shining in your sea,
stars in your sky,
wildflowers in your meadows.

this day is yours

this day is yours
to love
to hope
to make beautiful things
to laugh
to start again
to make it what you want it to be
don't believe it is too late
to dream new dreams
to fall in love again
to wish upon a star
to be who you are

work of art

your feet dance
with every step,
drawing you closer
to the place where you belong,
where you are free,
and from your lips melodies
and poetry burst and create
songs of delight
and your eyes are mirrors
of light, of glory, of stars,
of everything
beautiful and bright;
every bit of you
is a work of art.

your heart is a flower

your heart is a flower:
water it daily with joy,
with songs, with cotton candy skies,
watercolor sunsets
and kind words.
let the light find you
and make sure the sun
shines on your heart
and watch it
bloom.

loved, so loved

i want to be wild,
to leave trails of stars and spring
and rain and light and glory behind me.
to never settle, to never forget
who i am, who i was, who i'll be,
who made me and why my heart beats.
to let the sun make my soul its home,
to let freedom run in my blood,
to look at the sky and to find the stars smiling down at me.
to let drops of rain soak me,
to feel, to know that i am alive,
that this heart of mine was meant to beat,
to believe that i am loved, so loved
and to know that my eyes were meant to see glory.
to know that the darkness does not own me,
to know in my heart, my soul, my bones, my inmost being
that i am a child of the Light, a daughter of the sunrise
and loved, so loved.
that this life of mine was made on purpose,
that my eyes blink and i breathe and my feet walk
and my heart loves because it is what i was made for.
to know that i am not a mistake, i am not a failure.
i am my dreams and my laughter and my tears and
my hopes
and i am loved, so loved.

songs of beauty, stories of hope

the stories we will tell
are being written today.
the songs we will sing
are composed of these little moments.
may bravery and redemption
be tangled up between our words,
may they be the music of our songs.
let us be songs of beauty,
stories of hope.

the past is not yours

stop swimming
in the ocean of shame,
of guilt, of regret.
let grace be your lighthouse
and swim to its shore.
let yesterday drown
in the sea of forgetfulness
and let go.
the past is not yours.

gaby comprés

make room

make room
in your heart
for the beautiful things,
make room for light,
for love,
for glory and hope.
let your heart be their home.

goodness

there is goodness in starry nights,
in the light that touches the clouds at sunset.
there is goodness in the laughter
of children, in the music their lips sing.
there is goodness in your outstretched hands
as they hold broken hearts.
there is goodness in the wind
that takes away the pain
and brings rains of joy.
there is goodness in your heart,
there is goodness in you.

gaby comprés

and a love

dreaming of coffee dates
and your hand crawling towards mine
and a love
dreaming of watching sunsets
next to you, and your fingers tangled in my hair
and a love
dreaming of you, singing songs in my ear
and a love
dreaming of the way your arms
will feel around my waist
and a love
dreaming of your eyes, lit up by your smile
and a love
dreaming of not wanting to hide from you
and a love
dreaming of a love
and a love
and a love.

see me

see me
the way i
see myself
with the waves of the sea
in my hair
and their song in my swaying hips
see me
the way i
see myself
with flowers growing
in my heart
see me
the way i
see myself
with stars lighting up my soul
see me
the way i
am

gaby comprés

flaca

"tú si estás flaca."
  y estoy bella.
  y feliz.
  y llena de vida, con los ojos como dos estrellas.
  pero tú solo sabes decir
"tú si estás flaca."
  tú solo ves que estos huesos se han achicado,
  que mis muslos son más delgados,
  pero mírame.
  mírame bien,
  mira que mi alma es tan grande que no cabe en mi cuerpo,
  mira la luz en mi corazón,
  mira las palabras escritas en mi alma,
  mira más allá de mi piel.
  mírame,
  mírame bien, y dime
  que mi sonrisa da más luz que el sol,
  que me veo feliz,
  que he cambiado,
  que he florecido.
  son tantas las cosas que puedes decir,
  pero tú solo sabes decir
"tú si estás flaca."

skinny

"you are so skinny."
and beautiful.
and happy.
and full of life, with two stars instead of eyes.
but you can only say,
"you are so skinny."
you only see my bones,
my thinner thighs.
but look at me.
see me.
see how my soul has grown so much it doesn't fit in my
body,
look at the light in my heart,
at the words written in my soul,
look beyond my skin.
look at me,
look at me and tell me
that my smile is brighter than the sun,
that i look happy,
that i've changed,
that i've blossomed.
there are so many things you could say
but you only say,
"you are so skinny."

gaby comprés

with wild courage

i am not your words,
i am my own.
i am writing a story of grace and fire,
hope rising.
i am a flower,
i am a tree, rooted in my worth,
and i do not bend when the rains come,
i don't bow to the wind.
i stand,
tall and graceful,
with wild courage.

magic

magic is finding
the night sky in your eyes
when they light up.
magic is the sound
of your laughter
and the way
the wind dances
through your wild hair.
magic is the way you live,
with courage,
as if you have wings.
magic is the light
in your soul,
the love in your heart.
magic is
you.

you and i won't be forgotten

i never want to tire
of hoping
of believing
that these words are more than
just words
that this is not where it ends
that this is not all we have to give
that (you and i)
are so much more
than what we dream
that this story we are writing
(won't be forgotten)

you will bloom

listen to the music of raindrops,
singing,
"you are growing,
you are a flower
and you will bloom."

new year's resolution

find me braver
find me kinder
find me loving with
a wide-open heart
find me with flowers on my head
and forgiveness in my heart
find me alive
find me in love

if we fall

if we fall,
we shall learn to rise,
and we'll learn to love each other
just the way we are
and we'll turn the world around us
into something beautiful.
we shall tell stories
of love and hope,
and we'll look towards tomorrow
with light in our eyes
and if we fall,
we shall rise
and we'll turn the world around us
into something beautiful.

quiero siempre brillar

quiero siempre brillar,
ser una estrella en tu cielo,
una luz que no se apague,
un faro en tu mar.
tu luna en la noche,
y de día el sol.

let me always shine

let me always shine,
let me be a star in your sky,
an unfading light,
a lighthouse in your sea.
your moon in the night
and in the morning your sun.

poetry and a song

you are poetry,
you are a song.
you are eyes that rhyme,
feet that know where they're going.
you are words that don't stay silent,
you are an unwilting flower,
you are light that doesn't fade,
a heart that keeps beating.
you have beauty tangled in your hair,
and stars living in your eyes.
you have hope nestled in your soul,
and liberty written on your skin.
you have a song etched on your heart,
and heaven in your bones.
eternity is planted in your soul,
and redemption is a crown on your head.
you are more than gold,
more than dreams,
more than stars,
more than the sun.
you are poetry,
you are a song.

show me your heart

show me your heart,
show me the beauty you keep inside.
open your soul,
don't hide it;
let me see the light that shines within.
tell me your story,
tell me what makes your heart beat,
what sets your soul on fire.
tell me about your pain,
and know that it matters,
that everything about you matters.
know that your life is a gift,
that your life is grace.

let me be your home

let me be your home
let my hands hold your heart
and let my heart hold you
let me be your home
let me be your safe house
your shelter from the storm
let me be your home
let me be the place
where you learn to heal
let me be your home
let me be the wings
that carry you

Victoria's song

you will bloom.
you will burst up from the ground,
from a soil drenched in hope.
you will feel the rain touch you like a light kiss,
a promise from heaven that your spring is coming
along with the sun, bringing light to your soul.
you will bloom,
because victory hides in your name,
because even though the tough wind tried to kill you,
and the winter came and the earth shook
you did not,
and you will not be shaken.
your time is coming, and you will bloom.
and from inside you will burst color and joy and life,
a life that will tell your story,
a song of victory, of hope, of healing,
of a winter that ended, giving way to spring,
to joy and grace,
to wild love that flows like a river
making everything grow, blossom,
bloom.

how does the light get in?

how does the light get in?
(through) the cracks
the brokenness left,
through the doors of an open heart,
through the windows of a soul.
how does the light get in?
when (you) smile,
when hope is found.
how does the light get in?
when you wish upon stars,
when the sunlight touches your face.
how does the light get in?
through the words of a friend
and the kindness of a stranger.
how does the light get in?
when you let it.

lighthouses in the night

let our hearts
be lighthouses in the night,
guiding each other
carrying our souls
to shore.
let us be safehouses,
let us be libraries,
filled with poetry
and words of hope, grace
and new beginnings.
let us be songs,
lullabies that inspire
dreams and peace.

a garden

i will be a garden,
blooming and alive,
a home of hope,
a home of light.
firmly planted,
endlessly beautiful,
rooted in love,
growing in grace.

wildflowers

let's be wildflowers,
let our souls be scattered by the wind.
let us grow, wild and free,
tall and brave,
in the places that we dream,
in the places where our longings
are filled.
let us grow between the cracks
of brokenness,
and we will make everything beautiful.

en tus ojos aún hay luz

vida mía,
en tus ojos aún hay luz
aún hay magia,
en ellos hay vida,
en ellos queda la chispa suficiente
para iluminar todo a tu alrededor.
no te rindas,
no cedas,
aún no es tarde.
fuerza y luz te quedan
para volver a empezar.

in your eyes, there is still light

in your eyes, there is still light,
in your eyes, there is magic,
there is life,
there is a spark bright enough
to light up everything around you.
don't give up,
don't give in.
you still have light
and the strength to try again.

gaby comprés

you shine

shine.
for you are light
and wonder,
for there are galaxies
within you and
stardust
dances in your soul.
stars live in your eyes,
and glory and grace
live in your bones.
you are beautiful.
you are light and wonder.
you shine.

the words I want you to keep

everything is yours // for Gabriel

this world
and everything inside it
is yours
its beauty, its wildness
is yours
the birds sing for you
and every star in the sky
is for you to wish upon

light and grace

you are light and grace;
the stars wish upon themselves
to shine like you do.

i am made of

i am made of sunsets,
of cups filled to the brim
with coffee and milk.
i am made of children's laughter,
of giggles and play.
i am made of the stars
i wonder at in the night,
of flowers that grow
in my mother's garden.
i am made of books and poetry,
of words laced with hope and love.
i am made of light,
of music and silence,
of bravery and softness.
i am made of the song of raindrops,
of the promise that spring is coming,
that there is hope for me.
i am a song, i am a story.
i am poetry.

gaby comprés

stop hiding

stop hiding.
stop waiting for life to happen.
life is happening already
below your feet,
above your head,
all around you.
life is this moment.
stop waiting for your song to find you;
start singing.

85

this will be my life

this will be my life:
a dance of falling and rising,
of mistakes and grace,
a beautiful thing.
this will be my life:
filled with yellow and joy,
flowers and words,
love and light.
this will be my life:
seeking truth, seeking light,
seeking what's lovely,
seeking what's right.
this will be my life:
bittersweet,
sun and rain.
this will be my life:
a song of hope,
a story worth telling.
this will be my life.

let the stars write

let the stars
write our stories in the sky,
let them fill our days
with love and light.
let the stars
write poetry
of the moments we make,
let them turn our laughter
into bursts of light
that turn into ink on the pages
of the night sky.
let it be written in the stars
that joy will never leave us,
that the light will always shine for us.

you just have to dance

your heart is beating;
the music is already playing.
you just have to dance.

wonder

you are a wonder,
you are the pink in sunsets,
the light in the stars.
you are a wonder,
you are the waves of the sea,
the melody to my favorite song.
you are a wonder,
you are the rain that makes life grow,
the magic that makes winter turn into spring.
you are a wonder.

sunday afternoon

sunday afternoons were made
for sipping coffee
just for the taste of it
and reading poetry
while a soft song plays
sunday afternoons are for
sitting outside and watching the clouds
turn yellow and orange and pink

gaby comprés

your laughter // Rafa and Isa's song

your laughter
has become the song
that wakes my soul up.
your laughter
makes birds stop
and listen
your laughter
makes sunflowers yellow
and the sky blue.

when sunset comes

when sunset comes,
make sure to look out the window
or step outside
and as you see the light touching the clouds
and as the sunset turns into twilight
and the twilight turns into dusk
remember the beauty that hides in endings.
and when the morning comes
and the light wakes you up
as it floods your room
remember the hope
that comes with a new day
and that new beginnings
are on their way.

we are and we are and we are

i am and i am and i am
and i will always be.
you are and you are and you are.
and you will always be.
we are and we are and we are.
and we will always be.
dreamers.
singers.
lovers.
light.
fire.
art.
beauty.
poetry.
we are and we are and we are.
and we will always be.

promise me you won't sink

one day
we will be whole
but until then
we'll keep fighting,
we'll take one day at a time
we will laugh and we'll cry
and we will learn to take our walls down
we'll be a lighthouse to each other
and carry one another through the night
we'll see the sun rise
and we'll find the courage to try again
and the waves might try to drown us
but promise me
you won't sink

the words i want you to keep

this is the story i want in your hands,
these are the words i want you to keep,
the words i want to be yours as much as they are mine.
this is my heart, my soul.
this is what i want you to know:
that you are seen and loved,
known.
that you don't have to carry what doesn't belong to you:
the pain, the shame, the tears.
that the sun will rise tomorrow,
and hope along with it.

sunflower

may i grow
so tall and bright,
so free and wild,
so brave and vibrant
that when you see me
standing
you think i am
a sunflower.

buy yourself bright flowers pt. ii

"buy yourself bright flowers.
  buy them and keep them in your room,
  so that every time you see them you may remember that
  you're as bright and lovely as they are.
  buy them so that they remind you of who you'll be,
  of who you are:
  bright and bold and gorgeous and unfolding.
  buy them to remember that you too will bloom."

i wrote these words what feels like a million years ago, but
only a year and a half has passed.
i forgot them, these words and the flowers.
i forgot the holiness that hides in this small act,
this celebration of the Hope that is on its way,
the hope that things won't stay like this forever,
that goodness is coming,
that the work started on this heart will be completed.
but today i remembered.

the sound of raindrops

i carry the sound of raindrops
in my heart
like a song
a reminder
a hope
that i am not done growing
that the pain and the joy
are birthing me
and my bones are becoming
the earth
where my flowers will bloom

sister

sister,
let me be your blue sky, the color yellow,
and your happy song.
sister,
let me wipe your tears and put back the pieces
of your broken heart.
sister,
let me be the bed where you put your bones to rest
until you are ready to rise again.
sister,
let me hear the music of your laughter,
let me see you carefree and alive, let me hold your hands.
sister,
i miss the joy in your eyes, the sound of your voice,
the way you lived.
sister,
come home.

i want to sing to you

i want to sing to you
a song that touches your soul
and stays in your heart.
a song that gives you the words
your heart needs to hear,
a hymn to sing
when you don't know what to say.
a song the sparrows sing
when they come to wake you up,
and a lullaby for your dreams,
of hope and love.

love

in the end, this story you are living is all about love.
the love you kept,
the love you gave away.
the loving of yourself,
the loving of your lines and curves and broken pieces,
the love for the parts of yourself that you didn't always love.
the love for the parts of your story that made you,
and the love that you don't know yet.
the love that saved you,
the love that made you,
the loving of every bit of this life,
the love for the little things that made every day matter.

i don't want to hide

i don't want you to get lost
looking for me
i want to stand in the middle of your heart
to be the brightest star
i want you to see me
i don't want to hide

valley of wildflowers

don't be afraid of the rivers
that want to run free
down the earth of your face.
they will grow flowers and
turn your cheeks into gardens.
you will become a valley of wildflowers
and a land of milk and honey.

love yourself

write poetry to your soul
and use verbs like
(love)
 and adjectives like
wonderful and *precious*
and *enough.*
look at your reflection in the mirror and smile at it,
and laugh when you see your eyes shine
with the light of a million stars.
take (yourself) on coffee dates
and go on walks down your city
and get lost until you find yourself
along the way.
buy yourself dahlias and daisies
and put a few on your head.
maybe you will become a flower, too.

gaby comprés

six-thirty p.m.

the sun and i
go on a date
every day, at the same time.
six-thirty p.m.
we meet at the window in my room
and my eyes catch the last rays that
touch the clouds and then
my soul.

beauty // for Lo

beauty is your heart,
the words that you say,
the smiles you give,
the way you love this world
and its people
beauty lives in your name,
in your eyes,
in the story you are living,
in everything you are,
everything you do.

the perfect blend

coffee and milk
sand and sea
night and stars
flowers and rain
you and i—
the perfect blend.

love song

you are the stars in my sky,
the dandelions in my fields,
and the color yellow.
you are love letters
handwritten by God
and lighthouses in the sea.
you are the milk in my coffee,
you are the morning sun,
and the song the birds sing.

yellow // para Yomeli

i see you
and i see yellow
i see the sun and the stars
in your eyes
i see you
and i see yellow
i see a field of sunflowers
and you among them,
standing tall and bright
i see you
and i see yellow

red // para Andrea

i see you and i see red.
i see your fire,
your passion, your love.
i see you and i see red,
i see your taylor swift hoodie
and your radiant smile dressed
with red lips.
i see your heart,
the way you live bravely
and freely,
unafraid of falling, because
you know how to rise again.
i see you and i see red.

green // para Thalía

i see you and i see green.
i see the color of hope
in your eyes.
i see you growing,
not like a flower,
but like a tree,
strong and brave.
i see you and i see green.

blue // para Esther

i see you and i see blue.
i see a soul as wide and beautiful
as the sky,
a heart with love as deep as the ocean.
i see you and i think of peace,
of calm,
of a river showing the way to the sea.
i see you and i see blue.

gold // para Lulu

i see you and i see gold.
i see the sunset in your hair,
i see the way you move,
like the dancing flames
in your bonfire heart.
i see you and i see gold,
i see you shine,
i see you sparkle,
i look at the freckles in your face
and they become stars and glitter.
i see you and i see gold.

white // para Astrid

i see you and i see white.
i see you and i see the moon,
i see you shine
as you reflect the sun.
i see you and i see white,
you are a pearl,
a daisy,
a shooting star.
i see you and i see white.

rainbow

i see you and i see the rainbow.
i see you painting the canvas
of my life with your colors,
turning my days into a tapestry
of beauty and grace.
i see you and i see the rainbow,
i see promises kept and goodness filling my days.
i see you and i see the rainbow.

esenciales

se convirtieron en
mi sol
y la lluvia que me hizo crecer
se convirtieron en la canción
que mi alma aprendió a cantar,
en la melodía de mi risa
y las letras que no salen de mi mente.

in the most unexpected places

scatter the bits of my soul
like seeds
over wildflowers
so that i may learn from them,
so that i may grow in loveliness
and bravery
freely,
wildly,
in the most unexpected places.

rest your bones

rest your bones,
you are home.
lay down your ghosts,
the burdens you carry.
rest your bones,
let your wounds heal,
let the brokenness be made new.
rest your bones,
stop fighting grace,
stop fighting love.
rest your bones,
let yourself come home.

all the words

there will never be enough flowers
to fill the garden in your heart
and there will never be enough stars
to cover the sky that is your soul
and all the words
won't be enough to tell the wonder that you are
but heaven knows
i'll try.

every shining star // for Charissa

in a dark sky,
you are every shining star.
you are the spark
kindling every soul,
even when you fear your light
will go out.
you are a river,
filled with life,
showing the way into the ocean.

all that you are

i don't want
more than what you can give
and i don't want to
change your heart.
all that you are,
all that you'll be,
is all i'll ever need.

i am

i am
this glorious.
magical.
powerful.
thing.
i am formed by words
that don't exist.

the flowers that grew from your rain

i am not the remains
of what you left.
i am whole.
i was not left to die.
i am alive, thriving.
i am the flowers that grew from your rain.

people change

i stopped being the rain
and the sun
that gave you life
and i turned into wildflowers

i am the spring

if you and i were seasons
you'd be the winter
because i am the spring that came after you,
i am the fields of tulips and sunflowers,
tall and beautiful,
i am life blooming wildly and freely,
i am the seeds Hope planted,
i am evergreen.

call me complicated

call me complicated,
but how can i settle for less
than what i want?
call me complicated,
but i think you're just scared of me,
of the music my bones sing,
of the wildness of my spirit
and how my hair has a life of its own
i think you know i am too much of a woman for you
and it scares you

i want a life

i want a life
bursting at the seams with goodness, with color,
a life in which every day
is a cause for celebration,
a life that i never take for granted.
i want a life like honey; sweet and slow,
so that i may savor the richness that lives in my days.
i want a life
that teaches me, that fills me with hope and bravery
and kindness.
i want a life,
a life my own,
filled with my words and my mess
and love.

an 11:41 pm text that read, "you deserve love"

there are things
you think you know
but when the words come
from somebody else
their truth
(your truth)
becomes unwavering

the feeling you are not alone anymore

one day (or night)
it hits you
(the feeling that you are not alone anymore)
and even though you were never afraid of
(loneliness)
you don't want to feel it anymore

undress your heart

undress your heart.
slowly, softly.
gently.
for under it, lies beauty.
undress your heart.
know that your heart is fragile
and the undressing might hurt.
under your heart live
the most precious parts of you.
the diamonds and stardust.
undress your heart.
know that there is beauty in vulnerability.
undress your heart.
slowly. softly.
gently and boldly.
watch your light shine.
watch your joy brighten the sky
and turn it into a sea of lights.

i love you

i love you like this
like you are now
like you were
and like you will be
and i love you
i love you
like you are now
because your beauty is not in the shape of your bones
or the length of your hair
i love you
because of who you are and the way your heart beats
and i love you
because when you smile your eyes close
because your light is too bright
i love you
like you were
because your heart loved gently and wildly,
because you knew your story was one worth telling even
though you couldn't see it
and i love you
i love you
like you will be
because i see you fighting for goodness, holding on to the
hope that better things are on their way
i love you
because you look towards tomorrow with light and hope
and i love you
like this
like you are now
and like you will be

daughter

i'll name you after a flower
and i'll let raindrops fall on your forehead
so that you bloom
i'll plant kisses
like daisies on your cheeks
so that you become a garden
and i'll sing to you my love
so that you never forget the words,
so that you never doubt you're loved
and i'll write to you
words i don't know yet
i will reach to the sky
and bring down stars
to teach you to shine like they do

en la luz

tú no tienes miedo de ser,
de sentir, de vivir
lo que eres.
y no vives la vida; ella te vive a ti.
tú no te dejas esconder,
estás en medio de todo,
entre las flores amarillas, las rosas rojas y los atardeceres rosas;
tú estás en las olas del mar,
danzando y nadando en aguas de gracia,
estás en las estrellas, en el sol,
estás en la luz.

in the light

you are not afraid of being,
of feeling, of living
what you are.
and you don't live life; she lives you.
you are color, you are joy.
you don't hide;
you are in the midst of everything,
between yellow flowers, red roses
and pink sunsets.
you are in the waves of the sea,
dancing and swimming
in waters of grace.
you are in the stars,
you are in the sun,
you are in the light.

life and light

as long as we're alive
you and i
we'll fight against the fading of the light
as long as we are here,
making, creating, living,
moving, laughing, singing,
darkness won't find a place to stay,
for life and light will flood every room in our hearts
every step we take, every word that leaves our lips,
feeds the burning fire in our souls
as long as we're alive,
as long as we're here,
darkness will flee
and the light won't fade.

the house where hope lives

my bones are the earth
where flowers grow,
my eyes are the night sky
filled with stars.
my skin is a canvas painted with glory, a picture of grace.
my body is the house where hope lives,
my heart is the place she stays,
making room for the better things she knows are on the way.

this wild hope

it is this wild hope,
this wild love
that keeps my heart burning
it is the certainty that tomorrow will not be like today,
that the birds will sing happy songs for us
it is this wild hope
that makes my words of love flow like a river to the sea,
and it is this wild hope that makes my love turn into rain,
rain that waters your dry land
and makes your garden grow,
it is this wild hope that grows like wildflowers in my soul,
like spring after winter.
it is this wild hope
that i hold on to.

feeling alive

feeling alive feels like
yellow flowers growing in my bones
and blooming on my skin
it feels like the sun rises
not in the east
but from within me

poetry

the magic of poetry.
is that it makes everything
beautiful.
it fills your lungs
like air.
it turns your soul
into a sky full of stars.
your heart
a field of wildflowers.
you.
into a poem.

keep these words

i hope you keep these words—
these breaths i give every time my fingers type,
these beats from my heart,
these children i've birthed,
these stars i've thrown into your skies:
they are the life i want to give you,
the stars that guide you home.
i hope you keep these words-
write them in your heart,
write them on your skin,
keep them in your soul.
sing them to your tired bones
till they begin to dance.

gaby compres

thank you

this book wouldn't exist if it weren't for the amazing friends, cheerleaders, and encouragers that exist in my life. i will never have enough words and pages to thank you for all you do. but i shall try.

thank you to Charissa, for simply being the best. thank for believing in these words and for believing in me, for taking the time to read and edit this collection. you are one in a million, the brightest star of my sky.

thank you, Taylor Mabelitini, for helping this book come alive with your art.

gracias a Beatriz Sang. este libro probablemente no existiría si tú no me hubieses preguntado después de clases: "¿y cuándo tú vas a escribir otro libro?" gracias por ser una inspiración.

thank you to my beautiful friends and sisters: Yomeli, Andrea, Esther, Thalía, Lulu y Astrid. you are my rainbow and a million prayers answered. thank you for the color and the joy you bring to my life. gracias por creer en mí, por inspirar tanto de lo que está en estas páginas, por quererme a mí. las amo.

gracias a mi familia: mami, papi y Diego. si yo soy un árbol, ustedes son mis raíces. los quiero mucho.

thank you to Georgina. there are no words for all that you mean to me. i love you all the way from here to China. this book is for Giara and Gabriel. never doubt your worth.

the words i want you to keep

thank you to the big sister i never had, Laura Concepción, for always believing in me. love you always.

thank you to the lovelies Casey Van der Stel & Claire Busler. both of you were light in a moment of darkness for me. you shine with the light of a million stars. you are what joy looks like. i love you both.

thank you to Jennifer Legra and Rafaella. you both mean so, so much to me. i am trying not to cry as i write this. Jen, thank you for believing in me and my words. Rafaella, i love you, muchachita. you inspire me every day. i could write a thousand poems about your laughter. may you always shine and be brave.

thank you to Lo Schubilske, for always being on my side. you are a treasured friend and i am so glad that you are a part of my life. you breathe beauty and loveliness.

thank you to Nicole Lee. every page in this book is for you. i read this quote the other day, and it said, "make new friends, but keep the old; those are silver, these are gold." you are always gold.

thank you to Daelynn and Danaya. two more perfect and beautiful sisters have never existed. i love having you and the art you make in my life.

thank you, gracias, Marleigh y Elizabeth. i love how you've let my words and i be a part of your beautiful friendship.

thank you to all the friends i've made on the internet: Caryn Jackson, Annika, Ella Stettner, Rachel Hankinson,

gaby comprés

Breton Anderson, Estella Dentinger, Nadine Moraleja, Elizabeth Prisby, Caitlin Lassiter, Brianna Bischof, Lily Garay, Francina Herasme and Robert Mentes (among many, many others): thank you, from the bottom of my heart for all the kind words of encouragement you've sent my way. how lovely it is to know that my words are loved by you. this book is for you all.

thank you to the wonderful friends i have met over at the *impractical dreamers* group: Jordan Gage, Emily Lorin, Natasha Rulason, Rachel Haas, Ashley Sapp, Bethany Morris, Jessica Thornton, Micaela Evans, Lauren McHugh, Lauren Woods, Colleen Sullivan, Kaitlin Kline, Tawni Sattler, Brooklyn Smith, Kallie Shirley, Jasmine Vakharia, Sarah Fisher, Kalee Sokolowski, Chrissy Horansky, Natalie Wise, Kayla Hollatz and Cydney Irby. the brave way you live your lives inspires me. i am so glad have all of you to look up to, artists and dream chasers and bright lights.

thank you to Valentina, who makes me smile when she retweets my poems. it means more than you know.

thank you, God for all of this: the words, the people, the inspiration. thank you for your goodness and grace, your mercy and love. all that i am is found in You.

and, lastly, thanks to you. thank you for reading these words. they were written for you. this book wouldn't matter as much and carry all this worth if it weren't for you.

about the author

Gaby Comprés is a twenty-something poet from Santo Domingo, Dominican Republic. Inspired by nature, people and her own experiences, she has been writing poetry since March 2014. Her work has been published in several magazines, including *Grafted Magazine* and *Majesty*. She published her first poetry collection, *A Song of Bravery*, in March 2015, at the age of eighteen. When she is not writing, she is reading and drinking coffee.

Made in the USA
Monee, IL
17 July 2022